DEDICATION

This book is dedicated to the men and
women who dare to stand against the
devices and traps of the enemy.

D1441339

CONTENTS

ACKNOWLEDGMENTS

FIRST, I AM forever indebted to my spiritual mentors and my parents, Pastor Edward and Dr. Alice Johnson. They have played an instrumental role in my life's path and I want to thank them for their wisdom, insight, and immeasurable love. Additionally, I would like to express my appreciation to my bishop, Maryann Maybanks, for the many years she spent seeding positive words into my life.

To my church family, I want to say thank you for the unwavering support along my journey and for helping me follow the ministry path the Lord has etched into my life.

To my lovely children, Edward and Krystal, thank you for showing me the true definition of unconditional love. It is through you that I became anchored and realized my true mission in life: to be a well-rounded father and a man of God.

Finally, I would like to express my deepest gratitude to my lovely wife, Amber. Without her continued love and never-ending encouraging words, I would certainly not be the man I am today. Thank you for always believing in me, even when I didn't, and for pushing me to be the man of God I am today.

INTRODUCTION

THERE ARE MANY so-called experts in demonology or spiritual warfare. However, a distressing number of these "experts" have never come face-to-face with an actual demonic attack or even had any contact with the spiritual realm. The information they share, if accurate at all, comes from third-party sources and not actual experience.

I wanted to write this book to share my actual experiences in this realm. As a minister of the gospel, the Lord has allowed me to witness the demonic realm up close and personal in order to increase my effectiveness in sharing the gospel. This is a key point. The demonic realm is real, but battling it is nothing to brag about. Christ brings the victory and it is His power, His victory that needs to be bragged about. The war is over the souls of men, and the demonic realm is but one battlefield among many.

Looking back at my life and, in particular, my childhood, it is obvious how God has brought me to this point. My introduction into the spiritual realm began when I was six years old. My parents and I came home one Friday evening from a church service. As was our custom, I went upstairs to bathe and change for bed. After finishing, I came downstairs for a time while my parents remained upstairs in their room. The lights were off and deep shadows played in the corners of the living room. I sat down on the couch for a time until called upstairs by my mother, but just as I reached the foot of the stairs, I felt a strange urge to look back at the couch.

What I saw has stayed with me ever since. A glowing man dressed in a white robe sat on the couch looking back at me. Naturally, this terrified me and I ran upstairs as fast as my legs could carry me. At the top landing, I glanced back, hoping my imagination had dispelled the glowing man.

The man now stood at the foot of the stairs staring up at me.

I gasped in fear and darted to the safety of my parent's room. I never told them about this incident. I feared they would dismiss it as the overworked imagination of a six-year-old boy.

The next incident began when I was eleven years old. For the next two years, I underwent the most horrific and traumatic experience of my young life. Every night at some point I would be mentally assaulted by the most profane and evil thoughts. Profane words would spring into my mind like a torrent of evil washing over me, lasting sometimes for up to three hours.

Unless you have experienced something like it, you can't imagine how much in fear I lived. I hated going to sleep and would frequently wake up after a long night battle, exhausted and feeling defeated. I don't know where this obscene language and thoughts came from. I lived in a godly house and was being raised by godly, born-again parents. I just wasn't around such foulness even at school.

I would always pull the covers over me like a shield, regardless of how hot it might be inside my bedroom— even during the summer days when pulling the heavy blankets over my head made me sweat profusely. But I felt like I needed some barrier, something that would ward off these attacks.

For two years, until I was thirteen years old, I suffered

these nightly mental attacks. I never told my parents. I didn't want them to think I was crazy or just imagining things. However, it didn't stop me from thinking I was nuts! I had no friends and the teens my age at church generally avoided me because we were poor by society's standards. My parents taught me about God and that I was to love people regardless, so I never held their avoidance of me against them. But in the end, I thought I was losing my mind. What other options did I have?

Many years later, I can now look back on that time and realize that God was preparing me for something greater. As a child, I did not realize this. I hadn't matured spiritually enough to make the connections. This is why it is so important to pray for your children and to listen to them. Be careful not to dismiss your children's stories as an overactive imagination or even outright lies. They may be experiencing something spiritual that you are oblivious to.

I struggled to write this book, because this is the first time that I'm sharing my insights and my experiences of the spiritual realm. Even though I know who I am in Christ, I suspect there are those who have never experienced the spiritual realm as I have, who will dismiss my words out of hand. Regardless, I want to share with you my struggles and how the Lord has dealt with me over the years of my journey and battles with the demonic realm as well as to inform about the demonic realm.

There is a battle. There is a war. It is real. It is dangerous. And to win it, we need to be aware of it. *Demonic Warfare* is designed to make you aware of the reality of this war and to hopefully equip you with the spiritual weapons to defeat Satan and his minions.

Chapter 1
DEMONIC HIERARCHY

THIS BOOK IS not about the origins of demons, but you do need to be aware that the demonic world is the most organized system of government this world has ever seen. Lucifer, being only an angel—albeit a very powerful one—does not have the same abilities and power as God does. Therefore he is limited in the reach and scope of what he can do. He cannot be everyone at once. He cannot deal with everyone at once. To compensate, he has organized his demonic followers to assist in his plans.

Using a horde of demons under his control, he can observe you and monitor your behaviors, relationships, likes, dislikes, ambitions, lusts, and weaknesses. These observing spirits report to their superiors, and they in turn report to Lucifer. A plan of attack can be built around this information.

For example, I have witnessed people who testify of their health and strength, and then days later, their health is attacked. An observing spirit picked up on it and passed the information on. Perhaps the spirit detected a bit of pride in the testimony. Perhaps the spirit figured out that a person's faith depended upon such consistencies to be true in their life. And a plan of attack is conceived: destroy the health, destroy the faith.

Sound familiar? Job underwent a very similar attack. Everything was going well for Job (Job 1:1–5). He was rich, had good health, had a healthy family, had respect, and was an upright man before God.

1

Satan wanted to destroy his faith in God, not because he cared anything for Job, but because Satan hates God. However, the only way to hurt God is to hurt those whom God loves—us. If Satan could get Job to deny God, it would hurt God. If Satan can weaken your faith, then this is a victory against God.

As a believer under the protection of God, this attack cannot come unless God allows it. This can be of great comfort to believers, knowing that we are under God's protection. Nevertheless, God does allow these attacks. There are many reasons for this:

1. To build your faith

2. To prepare you for something else down the road

3. To be an example to unbelievers

4. To strengthen another believer's faith

5. To learn something about yourself

6. To demonstrate how much you need God

7. To show you the power of God

There could be many other reasons for God allowing Satan to challenge your faith, but regardless of the reason, God will not allow you to undergo an attack that you are not able to handle.

> There hath no temptation taken you but such as is common to man: but God is faithful, who will not suffer you to be tempted above that ye are able; but will with the temptation also make a way to escape, that ye may be able to bear it.
> —1 CORINTHIANS 10:13

This is a promise we can cling to, and it is a source of comfort when dealing with demonic attacks.

In Job's case, God allowed the attack against him (Job 1:12) and Job was up to the challenge. He never once sinned against God or charged God foolishly (Job 1:22). This should be our goal when we face demonic attacks. Greater is He that is in us than he that is in the world (1 John 4:4).

Demons are assigned to humans just to observe as that is their primary function. But it is not their sole function either. Ten years ago, I allowed my walk with God to lapse somewhat. I wasn't focused on the ministry aspect of my relationship with God as I should have been, and this fact was observed by the demonic observing spirit, passed up the chain of command, and eventually translated into an attack on my faith.

One night while asleep, I dreamed of a dragon attacking me. I woke panicked and drenched in sweat. I looked around the room to assure myself that it had only been a dream, and my eyes fell upon the dragon of my dreams. The lights were on so I could see it clearly. It filled the room with its body and it lunged forward, pinning my body to the bed with four incredibly strong arms. I could smell the stink and heat of its breath, and the musty odor of its body assaulted my nose and senses.

My heart nearly leapt right out of my chest. I couldn't believe what I was seeing. It was like something straight out of a sci-fi movie. Its presence filled the room, invading my mind and thoughts. I began to pray in my heavenly language. The Christ in me rebuked this evil spirit and it vanished as suddenly as it had appeared.

I told my parents and a few others of the incident; my parents and girlfriend at that time believed me, but most just thought I had an overactive imagination. But I knew the truth. I knew what had come to challenge my faith.

Sometime later, my mother, who is the co-pastor of the church I attend, taught a Bible study on spiritual warfare. In the midst of her lesson, the Lord reminded her of what I had told her about this attack and my description of the dragon that had attacked me. She then recalled another incident that had happened to me as a very little boy. I had drawn a picture of an imaginary friend and that picture matched the description of the demon that had attacked me. This was my assigned spirit—the one set to watch me.

He did more than watch me, but only because I had gotten out of line with the will of God and made myself vulnerable. God does have a hedge that He builds around believers, but you can walk away from that protection. You can remove yourself from that hedge by not aligning yourself with the will of God. When you do get out of line, your assigned spirit may step away from his role of just an observer and become your tormentor.

I have witnessed people coming to the altar of a church and telling stories of being attacked in their homes by spiritual entities. The pastor would pray and bind the spirit, but the evil spirit in your life will not return to its role of an observer until you are in line with the will of God. When you are in line with God, the evil spirit will have no choice but to become an observer because you are protected and it can't circumvent the hedge God sets around you.

When you get out of God's will, when a weakness becomes evident, the observing spirit may attack or it may bring in others to try and persuade you to yield to your weakness. Look at the following verses that describe the cooperation between spirits:

When the unclean spirit is gone out of a man, he walketh through dry places, seeking rest, and findeth none. Then he saith, I will return into my house from whence I came out; and when he is come, he findeth it empty, swept, and garnished. Then goeth he, and taketh with himself seven other spirits more wicked than himself, and they enter in and dwell there: and the last state of that man is worse than the first. Even so shall it be also unto this wicked generation.

—MATTHEW 12:43–45

Under normal circumstances, God has granted to each believer the discernment to recognize unholy and demonic influences in our lives. However, the observing spirit may go unnoticed as it is only observing and has been granted permission to watch.

Demons do have a hierarchy that they adhere to. It begins with an observing spirit and then works its way up the chain of command. Eventually, you may even come to Satan's notice.

There are two basic ways to be noticed by Satan. The first is to simply get out of God's will and become vulnerable to attack. The second one is to be upright like Job. In Job's case, God brought Job to Satan's attention as an example of what humanity is capable of—what God's creation is capable of. Satan wants to destroy such examples. He wants to prove that believers are weak and prone to betraying the God we claim to love.

Don't let that be you.

WHAT DOES THIS MEAN FOR YOU?

This means that there is an observing spirit watching you at all times. He has been assigned to you since the day you were born. He will report up the chain of command everything you do, everything you say, what you experience, how you react, and how well your relationships are going.

If you are a believer striving to obey God and live righteously, this information will be used to build a plan of attack against your faith. Remember, Lucifer isn't after you so much as he is trying to hurt God. The only way to hurt God is to use someone God loves—you.

Interestingly enough, an unbeliever or even a thoroughly backslidden believer may find themselves ignored by Lucifer. After all, such a person is already hurting God, why change it? But if you are seeking to walk with God, to have a real, dynamic relationship with God, then you will stir up the demonic realm. They will organize to thwart you if they can.

This is why it is so important for you to stay in God's protection. Anything God lets through to attack you can be turned to help you in some way. That is the greatest victory over Lucifer imaginable—when an attack by Lucifer turns into a tool for the kingdom of God.

When you are under attack, stay faithful. There is a reward and a blessing at the end.

Chapter 2
PROPHECY AND THE SPIRIT OF DIVINATION

THE FUTURE IS always tantalizing to us. We want to know the future and what the future may hold. The Bible contains much prophecy of things yet to come. The book of Revelation, for example, has been picked over and fought over for nearly two thousand years. We are fascinated by the future.

And yes, one of the gifts of the Spirit is prophecy:

> But the manifestation of the Spirit is given to every man to profit withal. For to one is given by the Spirit the word of wisdom; to another the word of knowledge by the same Spirit; To another faith by the same Spirit; to another the gifts of healing by the same Spirit; To another the working of miracles; to another prophecy; to another discerning of spirits; to another divers kinds of tongues; to another the interpretation of tongues: But all these worketh that one and the selfsame Spirit, dividing to every man severally as he will.
> —1 CORINTHIANS 12:7–11

God can grant prophecy to an individual!

However, there may seem times when demonic forces have the same power. They do not. It is important to understand the difference between prophecy and divination.

First, only God has the power to see into the future. Satan does not have this power nor do any of his minions. Second, what Lucifer has is spirits of divination. These two are different. Only prophecy can predict the future. Divination is something else altogether.

The Gift of Prophecy

There are many dimensions to the gift of prophecy, and not every prophet has the ability to utilize all the dimensions of prophecy. There are three classes or dimensions of biblical prophets. They are:

1. A prophet who is given a word of knowledge. This would be similar to Jeremiah and Ezekiel. These are often distinguished by the phrase, "Thus saith the Lord." God gave them direct knowledge of things to come and they wrote it down or preached it.

2. A prophet with the ability to actually "see" or "foretell" the future. The apostle John, for example, saw the future and wrote what he saw in the Book of Revelation.

3. A prophet who was only a messenger from God. Elijah might be an example of this. Elijah was sent by God to warn the wayward people of Israel, and he did his job well.

People with the gift of prophecy need to seek God diligently so He can tell them what dimension of the gift of prophecy they have been consecrated in. But don't mistake the gift of discernment for the gift of prophecy. They are not the same thing. Neither does it mean that because God used you to prophesy once or twice, you are called of God to be a prophet.

King Saul, for example, had the Spirit of the Lord fall

upon him, and he prophesied (1 Sam. 10:10–11). Saul, however, was not a prophet. He was called to be king. God used him only one other time to prophesy and that was to prevent him from killing David (1 Sam. 19:24). Neither incident made him a prophet. A preacher whom God uses to prophesy on occasion does not make that preacher a prophet—God can use anyone at any time.

Zacharias, John the Baptist's father, prophesied once in Luke 1:67–71. Zacharias, a priest, was not a prophet. He was called to minister in the Temple, but on that particular day, in front of that particular crowd, God used him to prophesy. Afterwards, Zacharias went back to being what God called him to be.

Those that are called to be a prophet have an office that they are called to fill. Much prayer and seeking of God's will is needed to determine which one of the three dimensions a prophet has been called to.

THE SPIRIT OF DIVINATION

In contrast to prophets, Lucifer has demons known as spirits of divination. These spirits collect data from other demons about people, places, and things that provide an accurate "right now" picture of what is going on with people, their finances, current trials and tribulations, and the state of their relationships.

> And it came to pass, as we went to prayer, a certain damsel possessed with a spirit of divination met us, which brought her masters much gain by soothsaying: The same followed Paul and us, and cried, saying, These men are the servants of the most high God, which shew unto us the way of salvation. And this did she many days. But Paul, being grieved,

9

turned and said to the spirit, I command thee in the name of Jesus Christ to come out of her. And he came out the same hour. And when her masters saw that the hope of their gains was gone, they caught Paul and Silas, and drew them into the marketplace unto the rulers.

—Acts 16:16–19

As you can see from the above scriptures, the divining spirit had knowledge of who Paul was. This knowledge came from the sharing of information among demonic forces.

Much like a charlatan, the spirit of divination makes predictions and guesses based upon an information gathering system. To the uninitiated, the sudden revelation of a fact may seem miraculous, but it is merely a means to deceive and distract you. They may seem like prophets, but they are merely charlatans.

These spirits have been observing human behavior and relationships for thousands of years. They are probably among the greatest psychologists in the world. They've seen it all. All they need to do is watch you for a while, and in many cases, they'll be able to accurately predict what may happen to you. It's just a trick. They have no real ability to see into the future, but they aren't stupid either. Just by watching, they can determine what may happen and even help orchestrate it because they know how you will react and behave under certain types of pressure.

Let's take a man who has anger issues. He gets upset easily when people try to correct him. An observing demon—a spirit of divination—can predict that he will have a "bad day" tomorrow and "suffer loss." You see, the divining spirit also knows that his boss at work is just about fed up with this man's temper tantrums. So all he needs to do is orchestrate someone to cross paths with our man who will correct him during work hours. Then the man loses his temper and the boss, fed up with it all, fires him, making the prediction come to pass.

In the spirit realm, there are two signals—for a lack of a better word—like spiritual airwaves. Think of the prophet like an old TV set with rabbit ear antennas. The prophet will catch the signals from heaven and relay the message locally. However, a prophet *must* be living right in order to catch the correct signal. If the prophet is just playing around or has sin in his life that has not been dealt with, then he won't be able to pick up the correct signal from God. He will counter interference or tune into the wrong signal altogether.

In fact, he may inadvertently tune into the second signal—a spiritual one, true, but one that originates with spirits of divination. Instead of getting right with God, I fear many prophets simply intercept the wrong signal and end up preaching the wrong message.

And in some cases, the prophecy may actually come to pass! But a prophecy that comes to pass may not be from God. It may not even be a prophecy...just a really good deduction. Look at the following verses:

> If there arise among you a prophet, or a dreamer of dreams, and giveth thee a sign or a wonder, And the sign or the wonder come to pass, whereof he spake unto thee, saying, Let us go after other gods, which thou hast not known, and let us serve them; Thou shalt not hearken unto the words of that prophet, or that dreamer of dreams: for the LORD your God

proveth you, to know whether ye love the Lord
your God with all your heart and with all your soul.
—Deuteronomy 13:1–3

The passage of Scripture above makes it very clear that
a false prophet can at times accurately predict the future.
This is not the same as actually being a true prophet. The
soothsayer in Acts 16 clearly made accurate predictions or
she would not have made any money for her masters. She
was good, but not as good as Paul was. Paul's receptors
were tuned into God, while hers were merely tuned into a
spirit of divination.

In Jeremiah 28, there is a story of a confrontation
between two prophets that disagreed about a certain
prophecy. One was Jeremiah and the other was the prophet
Hananiah. Jeremiah had been sent by God to predict the
fall of Jerusalem and the enslavement of its people by
Babylon. Hananiah had predicted that in two years God
would deliver Jerusalem and Israel from out of Babylon's
hands.

Think about it. Why would Hananiah make such a prediction? If he is lying, then he has only two years before
he is discredited and probably imprisoned and sentenced
to death for his false prophecy. In fact, his exact prophecy
was very specific:

> Thus speaketh the Lord of hosts, the God of
> Israel, saying, I have broken the yoke of the king of
> Babylon. Within two full years will I bring again
> into this place all the vessels of the Lord's house,
> that Nebuchadnezzar king of Babylon took away
> from this place, and carried them to Babylon: And
> I will bring again to this place Jeconiah the son of
> Jehoiakim king of Judah, with all the captives of

Judah, that went into Babylon, saith the LORD: for I
will break the yoke of the king of Babylon.

—JEREMIAH 28:2–4

Hananiah had to believe he had truly heard from God
to say something so specific. And perhaps the spirit of divination that gave him this prophecy was relying on the
fact that God typically delivered His people within that
timeframe, not believing that God really meant for Israel
to be enslaved for seventy years. Who knows what the
reason was for delivering this false prophecy to Hananiah.
Perhaps the divining spirit meant to discredit Hananiah
and destroy the hopes of the Jewish people when his
prophecy failed to come true. We just don't know. We do
know that Hananiah believed it and staked his entire rep-
utation on it, going so far as to publicly rebuke Jeremiah.

Regardless, Jeremiah prophesied Hananiah's death,
which came to pass within the year. It is a twisted story
about two opposing prophets. Hananiah's prophecy
never came to pass, but he believed it would. He honestly
believed, I think, that God had spoken to him. But he was
outside of the will of God. His receptors were not tuned
into Him and he intercepted the wrong signal.

It gets worse. When a prophet is attuned to the wrong
signal, there is a hidden carrier signal within that other
spirits can piggyback on and invade the life of the receptor.
Let's look at a passage already mentioned in a previous
chapter:

> When the unclean spirit is gone out of a man, he
> walketh through dry places, seeking rest, and fin-
> deth none. Then he saith, I will return into my house
> from whence I came out; and when he is come, he
> findeth it empty, swept, and garnished. Then goeth

he, and taketh with himself seven other spirits more wicked than himself, and they enter in and dwell there: and the last state of that man is worse than the first. Even so shall it be also unto this wicked generation.

—Matthew 12:43–45

Here we have a man who is receptive. He is not possessed, so to speak, he is clean of outside influences, but he is not tuned into God. He is just open to the first signal that comes his way. In this case, it is an unclean spirit.

But look what the unclean spirit brings with him! Seven other spirits more wicked than himself! Being opened and attuned to the wrong message invites many other things into your life that you do not want, even going so far as to deceive you completely by presenting themselves as angels of light (2 Cor. 11:14).

Being attuned to the wrong signal can create massive problems in your spiritual walk with God. In some cases, you may even believe you are walking with God when you are not.

Self-Proclaimed Prophets

Over the last few years, there have been more self-proclaimed prophets popping up than I have ever seen before in my life. The Lord has shared with me that the vast majority of these prophets have never been appointed nor commissioned by God. They are rogue agents of the kingdom.

In my walk, I have discerned that these self-proclaimed prophets have appended the title of "prophet" to themselves due to a very deep-rooted issue: low self-esteem. For whatever reason, when a Christian leader suffers from low self-esteem a need to be relevant builds. You want to be noticed. You want to be recognized. You want to influence people—all in an attempt to be relevant in the kingdom of God.

Prophecy is considered to be a mystical wonder, a powerful gift from God—after all, if you are called to be a prophet, God must have chosen you for something special, thus making you special and someone that should be followed, heeded, and respected. So you proclaim yourself a prophet of God, demanding that others heed you.

This insecurity and low self-esteem does not go unnoticed by the observing spirits that watch over us, and the information gets passed up to those spirits that can manipulate these fears and even allow you to tap into the wrong signal, making you believe your own false proclamation.

So many prophets today have just been manipulated into believing they are something special, something that others should respect, but they are not called of God. They are not prophets. They are not anointed by God. They are self-deceived charlatans, tapped into a beguiling spirit of divination.

In their desperation to be relevant and important, they have played a dangerous game. By assuming the office of a prophet without God's anointing, they have attracted spirits of divination, subjecting themselves to an ungodly influence that can destroy the very fabric of who they are.

I dare say some of you who are reading this fall into this category, but you are fighting it. You are resisting the truth even as the Holy Spirit is convicting your heart as you read this. You have convinced yourself that God has called you into this office, and this self-deception has begun to change you. As you give your ear more and more to the divining spirit instead of the Holy Spirit, the core of your being is being rewritten.

As a case in point, during the last two years, there has been an increase in homosexuality in the pulpit. Perversion has slithered its way into the lives of well-meaning men who, due to a lust for relevance and power, deluded themselves into thinking they were prophets, called of God. Harkening to a divining spirit can't help but change you. It is the nature of the evil spirits you are listening to.

The spirit of homosexuality is the frontline weapon against men. If the devil can pervert a man's masculinity into a feminine desire, he can never become the man of purpose God meant him to become. And if the devil can pervert a woman's femininity, then she will never know how to be a woman of grace.

When we mess with God's plan, try to steal divine offices for ourselves, we open the door to perversion and satanic influences on our lives. You may think you are doing something good; you may even convince yourself that you are doing the righteous work of God—but circumventing God only leads you into the direct path of the devil.

Think carefully on the following verses:

> Many will say to me in that day, Lord, Lord, have we not prophesied in thy name? and in thy name have cast out devils? and in thy name done many wonderful works? And then will I profess unto them, I never knew you: depart from me, ye that work iniquity.
> —MATTHEW 7:22–23

There will be many people—many people—who thought they prophesied in the name of Christ who will hear the words, "I never knew you: depart from me, ye that work iniquity."

It is no trifling thing to claim a divine office from God unless you are truly called. Are you called?

WHAT DOES THIS MEAN FOR YOU?

It means we are to try—put to the test—every spirit whether it is of God or not. Observe the following verses:

> Beloved, believe not every spirit, but try the spirits whether they are of God: because many false prophets are gone out into the world. Hereby know ye the Spirit of God: Every spirit that confesseth that Jesus Christ is come in the flesh is of God: And every spirit that confesseth not that Jesus Christ is come in the flesh is not of God: and this is that spirit of antichrist, whereof ye have heard that it should come; and even now already is it in the world.
>
> —1 JOHN 4:1–3

The "confession" that Jesus Christ has come in the flesh is the Scriptures. The Bible is our witness of Jesus Christ. God cannot and will not violate His own Word. Any prophecy either of your own or of someone else's needs to be scrutinized by the "witness," the Bible (2 Pet. 1:19–21).

If a prophecy that comes true contradicts the Scriptures, then it is not to be heeded (Deut. 13:1–3). This is the key.

Check your own heart. Are you in God's will? Are you walking with God? Are you attuned to God in the manner God wants? So many people want to be attuned to God, but they want to do it on their own terms. You can't do it that way. You must do it God's way. If there is sin in your life, if you are just goofing off, playing around with this thing called Christianity, then how can you be attuned to

God? And if you are not attuned to God, what then are you attuned to?

Put every prophecy to the test. Does it stand up to the Confessor? The verses below give you an idea of who the Confessor is. While the "confession" is the Bible, the "Confessor" is the Holy Spirit.

> Wherefore I give you to understand, that no man speaking by the Spirit of God calleth Jesus accursed: and that no man can say that Jesus is the Lord, but by the Holy Ghost.
>
> —1 CORINTHIANS 12:3

> Howbeit when he, the Spirit of truth, is come, he will guide you into all truth: for he shall not speak of himself; but whatsoever he shall hear, that shall he speak: and he will shew you things to come. He shall glorify me: for he shall receive of mine, and *shall shew it unto you.*
>
> —JOHN 16:13–14, EMPHASIS ADDED

Chapter 3

STDS: SEXUALLY TRANSMITTED DEMONS

THE SEXUAL EXPERIENCE between a man and a woman is more than a physical union. It is also a spiritual union. Sex is a union of body, soul, and spirit.

We are created in God's image, and God is a single deity that is of three parts: God the Father, God the Son, and God the Holy Spirit. If we are made in His image, then it stands to reason that we too would be made up of three parts: body, soul, and spirit. These three make up one person—you. They function in unity with each other just as the Trinity functions in unity with each other:

> For there are three that bear record in heaven, the Father, the Word, and the Holy Ghost: and these three are one. And there are three that bear witness in earth, the Spirit, and the water, and the blood: and these three agree in one.
>
> —1 JOHN 5:7–8

Each of your three parts operates in a different aspect of reality that, in all told, produce the human experience. The flesh or the body interacts in the physical world and the spirit interacts in the spiritual word. The soul, however, is the bridge between the two. But when two people have sex, there is a union between all three parts of both people that can allow the transference of demonic spirits from one person to another.

Yes, you read that right. In the same way that sex can allow the transference of physical diseases such as a chlamydia, herpes, and HIV from one person to another, sex can also transfer demonic spirits in a similar manner.

Sex is a deep physical and spiritual connection that allows emotions, physical feelings, and spiritual influences to be transferred from one person to another. If you are spiritually infected with a demonic spirit, sexual intercourse can infect your partner. You can transfer your struggles, your behaviors, and your lusts. The infection may be buried deep in your core—something you may not even realize is there. Only God can invade your spirit thoroughly enough to cleanse you from the inside out.

It automatically becomes perverted when we have sex outside of the bonds of marriage. This is clear:

> Marriage is honourable in all, and the bed undefiled:
> but whoremongers and adulterers God will judge.
> —HEBREWS 13:4

The bed, or the sexual act, is defiled outside of marriage, allowing for spiritual perversion. Unfortunately, this type of sexual perversion has become rampant in the body of Christ. Pastors are sleeping with women who are not their wives—even within their own churches—saints sleeping with other saints outside the marriage bond, and even saints sleeping with sinners. And we wonder why the house of God is consumed with everything but His true presence.

When two people connect with each other sexually, they open up a spiritual superhighway that allows spirits to be exchanged, just like body fluids are exchanged. This is wonderful if it is inside marriage and both individuals are wrapped up in the Spirit of God, but when there are other spirits involved, then the spiritual immune system is weakened.

Like it or not, disobedience to God is always a blow to your spiritual immune system. More than that, disobedience is an invitation to demonic spirits to influence and even alter your life.

But it doesn't stop there. There are saints who have sex with non-believers who have never experienced the Spirit of God in their lives. The only influences they have are the demonic spirits, and the moment you have sex with such an individual, you open yourself up to the influencing spirits rampant in the unbeliever. You contaminate your own spirit.

Is it any wonder those who do such things lose their joy, lose the thrill of the presence of God, lose the wonder of their salvation, lose the desire to submerge their lives in God's Holy Spirit? Contamination has happened, and once you are contaminated, you grow apathetic and uncaring for the things of God. Even reading this may have little impact on such an individual. My hope is that my Christian brothers and sisters will wake up before they get to that point.

No doubt some believe that a single night of sexual bliss is nothing more than a purely physical exchange. Some even justify it by claiming they have "needs." But let's say you go to a hotel, not even your own home, and hide your indiscretion away from your family, your friends, your loved ones, and those who are counting on you. You successfully hide it—though God sees all—and no one else knows. You have your night of sexual bliss and then return home. Know this, you do not return home alone.

Those demonic spirits that you opened yourself up to in your sexual pleasure will follow you home. You have granted them access to your life and to your home. You have granted them legal rights! If you were married and did this, your adultery has defiled your marriage. You bring those spirits into your home where they now have access to your spouse and your children.

You have slept with the enemy and then brought him home with you!

Sexually transmitted demons can be transferred through any sexual act—even masturbation—but certainly oral sex, pornography, inappropriate touching, or even inappropriate emotional exchanges that stir sexual desires and stimulate the bodies.

No doubt, there are many pastors and ministers who are gracing the pulpits of our churches who are infected with these sexually transmitted demons. No wonder they lack power in their preaching and their ministries are failing. Purity has been lost, and we have invited the demon into the heart and soul of our camp. We are compromised and need to get right with God.

It is sad to see a continual rise in the news headlines of pastors who fall due to sex-related crimes. The enemy is waging a war, and we have allowed him to infiltrate our very strongholds, the bastions of Christianity, the fortresses of our faith. We need to wake up.

What Does This Mean for You?

It means you must stay sexually pure. If you are not married, keep your body pure until marriage. You cannot afford to be infected with these sexually transmitted demons. They may spoil future relationships and even your future marriage. If you are married, stay pure to your marriage bond. Don't allow your mind, heart, and spirit to be corrupted and compromised.

A friend of mine told me this story: When he was a young man, he took over a stalled ministry from a man who seemed very godly and sincere, just overwhelmed. This pastor felt like he needed to step aside for his family's sake—a noble goal. What no one knew, not even his wife, was that while he had been pastoring—within the first few months of starting the church—he had a one-night stand with a woman who was not his wife.

He successfully hid it from his family, but in hiding it, he never dealt with it and the corruption began. Soon he did it again. This time, he formed a more lasting relationship, keeping a girlfriend on the side. Feeling guilty that he was a pastor and committing adultery at the same time, he resigned the church and gave it to my friend under false pretenses. My friend became the new pastor, and in time, this former pastor and his family actually came back to the church and joined it as members. During this time, he continued to have sexual relations with this other woman, again hiding it from his wife and children.

My friend found it difficult to pastor this man. This former pastor became distant, standoffish. Oh he was kind and generous, but he just never seemed to click with anyone at the church and kept his distance. My friend didn't know why, but that was because he didn't know about the man's dark secret.

This went on for ten years. Yes, you heard that right, ten years. This woman he was involved with eventually left him when he refused to leave his current wife, and so he found and took up with another woman. During that time, his wife never found out. The signs were all there, but she didn't want to examine them too closely. She didn't want to see the truth, and her blindness only aided his continual foray into adultery.

Then, ten years later, he finally had enough. He told his wife, "I don't believe in the God you believe in anymore. I'm tired of being a hypocrite. I'm not going to church with you anymore."

This seemed to come out of the blue for his wife. She was devastated. He went from a gospel preacher to a near atheist in ten years. How does that happen? Sexually transmitted diseases, that's how. He was infected and it changed him.

Though he had shrugged God off to appease a guilty and altered conscious, he didn't admit to his adultery right away. He even denied it. Two weeks later, he ups and leaves his wife, moves in with his girlfriend, gets a divorce, and cuts himself off from any of his old Christian friends.

But that wasn't the worst of it. His two oldest boys had become infected by the demonic spirits he had brought into his home. His oldest decided he also didn't believe in God, even though he grew up in church. The second oldest boy became addicted to pornography.

The whole family was plunged into tragedy. The only one rejoicing was Satan. This man dragged sexually transmitted demons into his home, never dealt with the infection, and destroyed his entire family. His outlook had so altered that he showed no remorse, no guilt, and no concern for those affected. He only thought of his own pleasures and needs.

How does one go from being a pastor to being morally bankrupt? In his case, sexually transmitted demons were the culprits.

It is not worth the price, my friend. Keep yourself pure. Sex is a superhighway that spiritual influences can transverse. In the marriage bond, it is a wonderful thing. Stay true to your marriage.

If you have already contaminated your spirit by having sex outside the marriage bond, then you need to allow God to do a thorough cleansing of your core being—from the inside out. Confess your sin, make it right with anyone around you that you may have contaminated also, and seek God. The longer you live with this, ignoring it, trying to hide it, the more it will corrupt your being, turning you into something you would never recognize.

Chapter 4
DEMONIC TRINKETS

IN WICCA, MOST spells and incantations almost always involve items as a point of demonic contact. Most witches and warlocks cast a spell over an object and then give the spelled item to the person requesting the spell. In some cases, if someone wants to cast a spell upon another person, the witch or warlock will cast the spell upon the item and instruct the person to place the object in the home or other personal space of the victim. The object will summon a demon to do the task laid upon it by the witch or warlock.

At first glance, you may think this nothing but a fairytale, something straight out of a movie. But it is true. It really happens. The main difference is that witches or warlocks have no special powers themselves. What they can do is task a demon to carry out a set of instructions. To the uninitiated, this may seem magical or powerful. It is not. It is merely a human playing at spiritual things they have no real concept of. They may think they are in charge, but they are not. As long as the spell or task is in line with the wishes of Satan, a demon may carry out the task. Don't be deceived. There is no power in magic that can supersede the Holy Spirit within us.

That doesn't mean we can't fall afoul of a spelled object that has a demonic force bound to it. Some years ago, my wife came across a rare doll at a consignment shop. She bought it and we were excited to give this to our eleven-month-old daughter. We did, but later that evening while my wife and I were watching TV, the Spirit of Christ in me became restless. I was somewhat confused as I didn't understand the cause of this restlessness. Finally, I got up to check on my daughter. She was sound asleep and everything looked peaceful. Still somewhat put out, I returned to the living room, but before I could really get settled, I knew I needed to return to my daughter's room. I did so in a hurry.

The moment I walked into her room, I saw a dark, shadowy figure hovering in the corner of the room. I immediately began to bind the demon, and it fled the house, going straight through the walls. I snapped the light on and the Lord affixed my eyes on the doll my wife had recently purchased. I knew I had to get rid of it. I took the doll outside and threw it away in a garbage bin. That small doll had been cursed with a spell, and my wife had inadvertently brought it into our house.

This can happen to anyone—even you. You need to be careful of what you buy or accept, particularly if you do not know the object's origins. You could accidently bring something demonic into your house, or worse, you could be the target of a spell.

A second way for an item to become possessed with a demonic spirit is to use the object repeatedly in a sin. Sin is an invitation to a demonic spirit, and the object most closely associated with that sin can then become the focus of the inhabiting spirit.

> The graven images of their gods shall ye burn with fire: thou shalt not desire the silver or gold that is on them, nor take it unto thee, lest thou be snared therein: for it is an abomination to the LORD thy God. Neither shalt thou bring an abomination into

thine house, lest thou be a cursed thing like it: but
thou shalt utterly detest it, and thou shalt utterly
abhor it; for it is a cursed thing.

—Deuteronomy 7:25–26

Idols and objects used for unholy purposes were cursed.
God warns us about having them in our house. Even
having them in our homes can bring the curse of the items
down upon us. They are things to be destroyed, not kept.

Most people might think that as long as they have
Christ, nothing can happen to them. That, however, does
not take into account our own wanderings. If we choose
to leave the protection of God, we can easily run afoul of
demonic influences. If we refuse to heed the voice of the
Lord, we can invite attacks into our lives. To this end, you
need to ask God for the gift of spiritual discernment—to
be able to discern the spirit of an item, person, or idea.

But the manifestation of the Spirit is given to every
man to profit withal. For to one is given by the Spirit
the word of wisdom; to another the word of knowledge by the same Spirit; To another faith by the
same Spirit; to another the gifts of healing by the
same Spirit; To another the working of miracles; to
another prophecy; to another discerning of spirits;
to another divers kinds of tongues; to another the
interpretation of tongues: But all these worketh that
one and the selfsame Spirit, dividing to every man
severally as he will.

—1 Corinthians 12:7–11

The Gift of Discerning of Spirits will allow you to discern what spirit is upon an item or person. The Spirit of
Christ is in you, as it is in me. When the Spirit of Christ

is not at ease, something is wrong. Something is not right. You need to determine what it is and get rid of it.

Unfortunately, too many believers tolerate this uneasiness. Eventually, you can sear your conscience, making it nearly impossible to avoid the attacks and pitfalls that demonic spirits will place before you.

WHAT DOES THIS MEAN FOR YOU?

When you accept Christ into your life, you will need to discard everything that reminds you of your past sinful life in order to maintain the freedom you found in Christ.

Doubts about your salvation come from a mind that is not guarded, that has yet to shed those things that enslaved you to sin to begin with. Until you get rid of those sinful trinkets in your home, you will not be able to adequately put on the Helmet of Salvation:

> And take the helmet of salvation, and the sword of the Spirit, which is the word of God.
> —EPHESIANS 6:17

> But let us, who are of the day, be sober, putting on the breastplate of faith and love; and for an helmet, the hope of salvation.
> —1 THESSALONIANS 5:8

> For he put on righteousness as a breastplate, and an helmet of salvation upon his head; and he put on the garments of vengeance for clothing, and was clad with zeal as a cloke.
> —ISAIAH 59:17

So many believers struggle with their own salvation, predominately because they keep around their home the trinkets they once used to indulge in sin. If the Lord delivered you from smoking, then get rid of the lighter and the ashtray. Don't keep them around the house. The spirit of that sin is still associated with the objects, giving it access to you, your family, and your home.

If you used to go to clubs, then get rid of the club gear. If you used to drink, get rid of the wine glasses or the shot glasses and the corkscrew! All the objects involved with your old sin must be removed as you have endowed them with evil spirits. They must go.

No wonder so many believers struggle with their salvation. They keep around the items, the objects, the paraphernalia that has been used in sin, allowing the spirits associated with them to continue to eat away at their minds and hearts. You say, "The Lord will protect me!" And so He has, by breaking you free from your addictions and sins, but it is not the Lord who is keeping those objects in your house. That is you. That is your choice. God has given you the willpower and the freedom to discard them—so get rid of them.

You also need to be careful what you let into your home. A couple shared a story how they wanted to help their niece who was having a tough time at her home, so they decided to let her move in with them. What they didn't know is that their niece listened to some of the most vile and abhorrent music imaginable. She listened to it on her portable MP3 player, quietly to herself. So no one really knew what she was listening to.

Strangely, within a few days of her moving in, the two youngest children began seeing a "bad man" down in the basement where the niece had been staying. The two little children became scared and refused to go down there anymore. It became so bad that they sought advice from their pastor.

Eventually, it came out what the niece was doing, but the girl refused to give up her MP3 player, so they asked her to return to her own home. By ridding their house of the MP3 player that was used to listen to such abominations, and by playing Scripture twenty-four hours a day down in the basement and binding the evil spirit, they were able to cleanse their house and the children eventually felt safe enough to go down and play in the basement.

You must get rid of the items attached to sin. Don't give demonic spirits access to your home, your life, or your family! Get rid of the things used for evil—for sin.

Chapter 5
IDENTITY CRISIS

THE ENEMY IS having a field day in the body of Christ. He is confusing our identities, homosexuality is on the rise among Christian men, the spirit of confusion and perversion is sweeping through the church like a plague, and our leaders are caught up in financial scandals or sexual scandals of one sort or another, including with underage girls and boys.

What's going on with us? Leviticus 20:13 gives us a pointed reminder of what God really thinks about such behavior:

> And the man that committeth adultery with another man's wife, even he that committeth adultery with his neighbour's wife, the adulterer and the adulteress shall surely be put to death. And the man that lieth with his father's wife hath uncovered his father's nakedness: both of them shall surely be put to death; their blood shall be upon them. And if a man lie with his daughter in law, both of them shall surely be put to death: they have wrought confusion; their blood shall be upon them. If a man also lie with mankind, as he lieth with a woman, both of them have committed an abomination: they shall surely be put to death; their blood shall be upon them.
>
> —LEVITICUS 20:10–13

It never ceases to amaze me how we rationalize and justify behavior that God clearly indicates is wrong. The church has begun to turn a deaf ear and a blind eye to this problem, refusing to hold leaders accountable for not discerning the spirits of compromise and perversion that have infiltrated into our churches. In our attempt not to be judgmental, we have granted sin permission to flourish. In trying not to upset people, we have created an environment where sin and all that comes with it can grow. In trying to love and accept everyone, we have condoned evil and wickedness—in the name of love. How is that love?

We've confused what it means to be a believer, a Christian. We no longer know what we stand for, what we believe in, what our purpose is. Our identity has become distorted and warped. We fight amongst ourselves, we tolerate sin—even going so far as to justify and rationalize why it isn't really sin, isn't really wrong. We've turned black into white and white into black, but when we are asked what color it is, we prevaricate, saying, "Maybe it's gray...?"

Add to this uncomfortable fact that most Christians identify themselves with a particular man or woman for what they believe and stand for—and not God—no wonder we are so confused. We are trying to live up to man's variable standards and losing our place in God. We need to break free.

> Now this I say, that every one of you saith, I am of Paul; and I of Apollos; and I of Cephas; and I of Christ. Is Christ divided? was Paul crucified for you? or were ye baptized in the name of Paul?
>
> —1 Corinthians 1:12–13

Christianity has splintered into groups, factions, and camps. We stand for what some man says, but few anymore stand in Christ. We harbor secret sins and hidden lusts. We have lost our identity.

And to that unfortunate environment, the enemy has unleashed his spirits of low self-esteem amongst our youth, blinding them to who and what they were meant to be. If the devil fears something other than God, it is the "future you" and what you may do for God. So he sows self-doubt, and with our leaders confused and splintered, the soil is rich for an ungodly harvest: insecurity.

One of the most powerful weapons the devil has in his arsenal is bestowing insecurity—self-doubt. This insecurity will plague you into your future, into your service for God, into your ministries, into the pulpits, into your marriage, and into your homes.

If the devil can make you insecure, he can keep you from feeling confident in the Lord. Once you lack confidence, you will be inundated with self-doubts, doubts that speak lies into your heart and mind, that promote evil urgings, and that paralyze your godly actions.

What Does This Mean for You?

The enemy is coming full force against the body of Christ because he knows that if he can alter your God-identity, then you will fail to become what God wanted you to be. This is his goal. If he can get you to abandon your God-identity, thereby sidelining you, then he has limited the effectiveness of the kingdom of God on this earth.

What is a God-identity? In essence, it is the purpose for which you were born—what God has called you to be. Regardless of whether or not you are called into the five-fold ministry (apostle, prophet, evangelist, pastor, or teacher), we are *all* called to be effective witnesses here on this earth.

> And he said unto them, Go ye into all the world, and preach the gospel to every creature.
>
> —MARK 16:15

> But ye shall receive power, after that the Holy Ghost is come upon you: and ye shall be witnesses unto me both in Jerusalem, and in all Judaea, and in Samaria, and unto the uttermost part of the earth.
>
> —ACTS 1:8

> Now then we are ambassadors for Christ, as though God did beseech you by us: we pray you in Christ's stead, be ye reconciled to God.
>
> —2 CORINTHIANS 5:20

The command to be a witness is not only for those in the five-fold ministry. It is for everyone. Each and every believer carries the Holy Spirit within us. It is our job to share the gospel with the lost and live a life that is honoring to Christ.

But if you allow the enemy to grip your mind, then he owns you. A preacher once said, "If the devil can get you to think wrong, then he can get you to do wrong." It all starts in your mind, in the area where we have established our identity. The enemy is after your thoughts.

> I beseech you therefore, brethren, by the mercies of God, that ye present your bodies a living sacrifice, holy, acceptable unto God, which is your reasonable service. And be not conformed to this world: but be ye transformed by the renewing of your mind, that

ye may prove what is that good, and acceptable, and
perfect, will of God.

—Romans 12:1–2

That the righteousness of the law might be fulfilled
in us, who walk not after the flesh, but after the
Spirit. For they that are after the flesh do mind the
things of the flesh; but they that are after the Spirit
the things of the Spirit. For to be carnally minded is
death; but to be spiritually minded is life and peace.
Because the carnal mind is enmity against God: for
it is not subject to the law of God, neither indeed
can be.

—Romans 8:4–7

Once the enemy has infiltrated your thoughts, your
identity becomes undefined, even altered. When this happens, it will take the power and might of God to remove
you from his clutches. It will require a transformation
back to the God-identity.

Don't allow your friends, family, and loved ones to alter
who you are in Christ. Don't conform to man's ideology of
who they picture you to be. Conforming to man's identity
is the same as conforming to this world. You need to be
what God created you to be.

Take a look at who you are. Are you who you are to
conform to some image other than Jesus Christ? It is His
image we are to conform to, not the world's image.

For whom he did foreknow, he also did predestinate
to be conformed to the image of his Son, that he
might be the firstborn among many brethren.

—Romans 8:29

Before you were ever born, God predetermined what He wanted you to be—conformed to the image (to identify with) of Christ. This is the only identity you need. The enemy and people will try to force you into a different identity. He will try to do so by sowing self-doubt.

Don't allow insecurity to change you. When you doubt yourself and what God has chosen for you to do, you have begun the process of being changed into something that is not Christlike. It may even seem good and noble, but anything outside of the will of God is not right.

Identify with Christ, not man.

Chapter 6
MUSIC

MUSIC IS PERHAPS one of the most debated subjects in the body of Christ. Music is everywhere. Everyone likes some kind of music. It is the only non-life-essential element that all of humanity enjoys. There may be a certain type of music you don't like, but there is some kind that you do.

Music pervades every aspect of our life from church to politics, from sports to fast food restaurants. We simply cannot live well without music! I dare say that every one of you has access to music, whether it is on an electronic gadget or an instrument you have lying around the house.

Did you know that there are more nerve endings in the ear than anywhere else in the body? It is, in all likelihood, the most sensitive part of the human body, and thus has the potential to have the most influence over your body. Music can relax us. Music can motivate us. Music can heighten fear. Music can increase anger. Music can bring peace. Music can stimulate health or cause the heart to beat out of rhythm.

Music is used in movies to create emotional responses. Imagine a horror film without music. It would be significantly less terrifying. Imagine the scene of major triumph without music. It would be less triumphant.

Fast food restaurants use music to increase their sales. Studies have been done that suggest that the faster paced the music is, the faster you will eat. The faster you eat, the more you can eat and the quicker you will leave, allowing someone else to take your place. They effectively use music to control your physical responses. Music is powerful.

Music is also good, but everything good that God has created, the devil has tried to pervert and change. Music that was meant to glorify God is now being used to glorify promiscuous sex, lust, drugs, alcohol, and everything else that is contrary to the Word of God.

Many Christians view all music as harmless. It's just sound, right? What harm is there in listening to it? It's not like I'm hurting anyone. What's the big deal with listening to secular music? The definition of the word *secular* should be a significant hint. *Secular* is defined as something denoting an attitude, an activity, or anything else that has *no* religious or spiritual basis. That alone should convince you.

Secular music, in addition, appeals to the flesh. We love the way it makes us feel, how our bodies can be in tune with it. It glorifies the flesh, not the God of the universe. That presents a problem.

Let me give you an example. If you take a frog and drop him into a pot of boiling water, he will immediately jump out, right? But if you take the same frog and put him in lukewarm water, he'll stay put. Indeed, he'll stay put as you gradually increase the temperature of the water to the boiling point. The gradual increase in temperature is not readily recognizable to the frog, and he stays contentedly in the heated water until boiled to death. That is exactly what happens to your spirit when you continue to listen to secular music. You may not notice that your spirit is being boiled, but it is. Slowly, gradually, your spirit-man begins to die. Your prayer life declines, your thinking changes, your behavior changes, and your desires change.

Christian music should challenge and encourage your

walk with God. It should point to Him, not you. Music is perhaps the most powerful tool on the planet as it is the only thing able to affect the body, soul, and spirit at the same time. Music was meant to unify these three parts of you in glorification of God. Secular music encourages your flesh-man, often feeding your lusts and passions. Instead of growing your spirit-man, your flesh-man grows, starving the spirit-man.

In Daniel 3, there is a story of three Hebrew boys who would not bow before Nebuchadnezzar's idol. What is interesting is that Nebuchadnezzar used music to try and motivate people to bow down and worship the idol. Apparently, he understood the power of music enough to utilize it in trying to affect the emotions and desires of the people. The three Hebrew boys had to not only resist the command, but they had to resist the impulse and spirit of the music.

King Saul in 1 Samuel 16:23 suffered from an evil spirit that plagued him. His relief came when David took up a harp and played godly music. This music brought peace, comfort, and drove away the evil spirit:

> And it came to pass, when the evil spirit from God was upon Saul, that David took an harp, and played with his hand: so Saul was refreshed, and was well, and the evil spirit departed from him.

Music has a hidden agenda that most people don't understand or even realize exists. The Lord explained to me that secular music is a bait and switch trick. You are lured in by one thing, only to be tricked into something else entirely. Secular music possesses hidden demonic inroads into the listener's life. The listener is then influenced by spirits of persuasion that pick away at their spiritual walls and attempt to conform them into something else entirely. The devil has created various genres of music to stimulate the emotions of the flesh. As an example, music like R&B stimulates the sexual appetites of the flesh and heavy metal stimulates the aggressive emotions of the flesh. Most preachers are afraid to tackle this subject because they too are lovers of secular music. Indeed, much of the music played in our churches resembles secular music in so many ways. Often, the only difference between Christian music and secular music is the words. The music itself is the same, and the people who sing this so-called Christian music often look no different than their secular counterparts.

It is impossible to listen to secular music and have a growing, thriving relationship with God. They are mutually exclusive. Secular music uplifts the flesh, the enmity against God.

> Because the carnal mind is enmity against God: for it is not subject to the law of God, neither indeed can be. So then they that are in the flesh cannot please God.
>
> —ROMANS 8:7–8

Music that puts you in the flesh means you cannot please God. The Bible also says:

> And be not conformed to this world: but be ye transformed by the renewing of your mind, that ye may prove what is that good, and acceptable, and perfect, will of God.
>
> —ROMANS 12:2

41

You can't contaminate your body with secular music and assume that you are filled with the Holy Spirit. It's impossible! How can you be filled with the Holy Spirit while you are filling yourself with fleshly music? The two are incompatible. They cannot co-exist. When the Holy Ghost is absent from your life, having been quenched, your spiritual immune system is severely weakened, making you vulnerable to spiritual attacks. Before long, you may even lose your anointing.

It is not OK to think that you are in right standing with God while you are listening to secular music. This is the season in which God will enforce His Word and the truths contained therein. If you have contaminated your body with secular music, then you have quenched the Holy Spirit inside of you. The two cannot cohabitate.

> Quench not the Spirit.
> —1 Thessalonians 5:19

The Lord has granted me permission to say that any pastor that condones, tolerates, or encourages the flock to listen to secular music is under a curse from God. Music is one of the main reasons we have seen a major decline in God's presence within our churches. There is a spirit there, all right, but it is not the Holy Spirit of God.

And don't think that the so called "oldies" and "goodies" are necessarily any better. Any music—any music—that does not glorify God is secular. All secular music that glorifies the flesh will contaminate your spirit and allow entrance to spirits of persuasion that is against God.

WHAT DOES THIS MEAN FOR YOU?

In short, it means you must get rid of all the secular music in your life. You can't control what others do, but you can control what you voluntarily listen to. You can control the music in your house. You can control the music in your car. You can control the music you put on your various electronic devices.

I'll tell you what is probably the main reason you will have a hard time letting go of your secular music. Likely, you have spent hundreds, if not thousands, of dollars on your secular music. Trashing all that money is hard for most people. Because you have invested so much money into it, you have placed your heart on it.

> For where your treasure is, there will your heart be also.
>
> —MATTHEW 6:21

Your music has become sacred to you since you have invested so much money into it. Throwing it away will mean severing your heart from it, a traumatic experience for most. You won't let go, because your heart is too attached to it.

You're going to have to trust God in this matter. Don't justify secular music in your life. Don't rationalize it. Just get rid of it. You need to rely upon God. You need to invest in godly things so that you can easily detach yourself from secular music.

Pastors need to lead the way in this. Perhaps you should have a music CD burning Sunday or an iPod erasing Sunday. If you want the Holy Spirit's power back on your life and on your church, then take a stand against secular music. Bring your music to the altar and give it up to the Lord.

Resist it. Refuse, as the three Hebrew children did in Daniel, to dance to it, to walk to it, to nod your head to it, to succumb to it in any fleshly way, or to bow to it. You can't escape the music as you go out into the world, but you can certainly resist it. You don't have to give permission to the flesh to bow to it. Don't worship secular music!

All music is spiritual. What is the spirit of your music? What is being invited into your life by the music you listen to? What are you inviting into your family's life by the music you listen to?

Chapter 7
FRIEND SOUL-TIES

Can two walk together, except they be agreed?

—Amos 3:3

THAT IS A good question. How can two people walk together if they are not in agreement? How can two people work together who are not in agreement? In general, it is impossible. There has to be some form of agreement in order to move together and accomplish something together.

While growing up, I made friends with a couple of boys in the neighborhood who were not saved. I assumed that as long as we never did anything sinful, everything would be OK. After all, there were plenty of things boys could do that didn't involve sin. I couldn't have been more wrong. Being around them and listening to them talk, tell jokes, and speak of other people strained my Christianity in ways I never expected. I found myself fighting my flesh and all the accompanied desires as I was exposed to their desires and passions. Later, I discovered I had been fighting spirits that were on my "friends."

It is important to realize that anyone we spend time with is not isolated spiritually. All of us carry spirits with us and they impact those around us. When ungodly spirits accompany your friends, you cannot help but be affected in some manner. Their mannerisms, their likes and dislikes, their attitudes toward authority, women or men, their passions, and even their humor all begin to rub off on you as you spend time with them.

I never went to a club, drank alcohol, or smoked. However, I found the spirit of curiosity trying to invade my "God" space, producing an internal struggle. It may be subtle at first, even innocent looking, but the longer you are exposed to these evil spirits, the greater the internal struggle becomes and the harder it is to discern which is which.

No matter how anointed you think you are, you are susceptible to these influences if you hang around them. You cannot handle thorns and expect not to get pricked. God warns you not to yoke yourself with unbelieving friends— casual friends or even the more significant boyfriend or girlfriend.

> Be ye not unequally yoked together with unbelievers: for what fellowship hath righteousness with unrighteousness? and what communion hath light with darkness? And what concord hath Christ with Belial? or what part hath he that believeth with an infidel? And what agreement hath the temple of God with idols? for ye are the temple of the living God; as God hath said, I will dwell in them, and walk in them; and I will be their God, and they shall be my people. Wherefore come out from among them, and be ye separate, saith the Lord, and touch not the unclean thing; and I will receive you. And will be a Father unto you, and ye shall be my sons and daughters, saith the Lord Almighty.
>
> —2 Corinthians 6:14–18

Look at the questions that are asked:

1. What *fellowship* hath righteousness with unrighteousness?

2. What *communion* hath light with darkness?

3. What *concord* hath Christ with Belial?

4. What *part* hath he that believeth with an infidel?

5. What *agreement* hath the temple of God with idols?

The obvious answer is none. So how can you walk with an unbeliever? How can you expect to fellowship with them? There is only one way.

You have to find something you agree on.

And that is the danger. What is there that you can agree on? Anything you settle on is so ridiculously narrow that nothing significant can be built—unless you compromise your spiritual walk with God. In order to do that, you have to open yourself up to the spirits that they have accepted into their own lives.

When you attach yourself to people who are not saved, you open yourself spiritually to connect with them. Once that connection is made, demons gain legal rights to pass through that connection to you and your home.

This is called Transference of Spirits. It is very real, and you will find yourself acting and talking like the other person, because not only have you bonded on the fleshly level, but you have bounded on the spiritual level.

There are, obviously, two different types of Transference of Spirits listed in the Bible. One is holy and the other is unholy.

Holy Transference of Spirits

The very first transfer of a spirit came from God when God breathed into Adam the breath of life and man became a living soul:

> And the Lord God formed man of the dust of the ground, and breathed into his nostrils the breath of life; and man became a living soul.
>
> —Genesis 2:7

The word *breath* is also translated in other places as the word *spirit*. You could say that God breathed into Adam the *spirit* of life. This was a holy transference of a spirit to Adam.

Another example of a holy spiritual transference is when God took the spirit of Moses and gave it to seventy men in an effort to help Moses with ruling the people of Israel:

> And the Lord said unto Moses, Gather unto me seventy men of the elders of Israel, whom thou knowest to be the elders of the people, and officers over them; and bring them unto the tabernacle of the congregation, that they may stand there with thee. And I will come down and talk with thee there: and I will take of the spirit which is upon thee, and will put it upon them; and they shall bear the burden of the people with thee, that thou bear it not thyself alone.
>
> —Numbers 11:16–17

Indeed, Elisha understood that this was possible, and when Elijah asked him what he wanted, he asked for this:

> And it came to pass, when they were gone over, that Elijah said unto Elisha, Ask what I shall do for thee,

before I be taken away from thee. And Elisha said, I pray thee, let a double portion of thy spirit be upon me.

—2 KINGS 2:9

Elisha wanted a double portion of the spirit that was upon Elijah. This explains why he was so determined to go wherever Elijah went. He understood that by walking with Elijah there was a good chance Elijah's spirit would rub off on him. By walking in agreement, Elisha saw the fulfillment of his wish. He performed exactly twice as many recorded miracles as Elijah did.

UNHOLY TRANSFERENCE OF SPIRITS

In like manner, an unholy transference of spirits can occur. Notice the following verse:

Looking diligently lest any man fail of the grace of God; lest any root of bitterness springing up trouble you, and thereby many be defiled.

—HEBREWS 12:15

The spirit of bitterness can be transferred to another and they can be defiled by it. When you walk with an angry person, you may take on angry attributes (Prov. 22:24). Scriptures warn us over and over about walking with people who have upon them an evil spirit, for that evil spirit can be transferred to you.

There are several ways to attract an unholy transference:

1. *From the crowd or group.* In Acts 13, a group of honorable men and women were stirred up by a crowd to persecute Paul. These were good men and women who allowed the

transference of hatred from a crowd to dominate their actions. If they had been confronted individually, outside the crowd, they may have acted differently, but the crowd overwrote individual sentiment and the spirit of the crowd controlled everyone.

2. *From gossip.* When you listen to gossip, you are naturally accepting what is being said and the spirit of that gossip automatically colors your judgment and attitude toward someone—even if you go out of your way to be nice, it is not a natural reaction. The gossip prompted an abnormal action. In 2 Samuel 15, Absalom spoke ill of his father, spreading gossip. In so doing, he turned the hearts of Israel away from David. The spirit of dissension and bitterness spread among the people.

3. *From authority.* Anyone who is in authority over you has the ability to transfer whatever spirit is upon them to you. In the Book of Esther, under the direction of Haman, the people were encouraged to slaughter all the Jews on a particular day. People who normally would not care or were even good people were suddenly now thinking of murder because the authority transferred the spirit of suspicion and hatred to the people.

4. *From soul-ties.* Soul-ties are bonds that you form with people. The yoking together of two individuals for whatever purpose. In 2 Kings 10, Jehu riding along in his chariot meets a man by the name of Jehonadab.

Jehu asks, "Is thine heart right as my heart is with thy heart?" Jehonadab answers, "It is." Jehu then asks him to join him in the chariot. Together they go off to fulfill the Word of the Lord. They had a soul-tie that influenced Jehonadab and changed his direction completely. Jehu's spirit of zeal was transferred to his friend. When you have soul-ties with unbelievers, their spirits will be transferred to you.

SECONDHAND SIN

The Lord revealed to me that some Christians attach themselves to sinners because they are addicted to secondhand sin. Oh, they don't necessarily commit the sin directly, but they choose to run with those that do. Instead of defying their friends' sin, they excuse it, tolerate it, or merely watch it.

Weak, lukewarm believers who are still friends with unbelievers try to live their sin through others. Some believers are just too afraid to indulge their own sinful lusts and desires, so they center themselves around those who do. They achieve a vicarious thrill through their friends—and even through the TV and movies they watch. Oh, they don't commit the sin themselves, but they sure don't mind watching it. They would never commit adultery, but they are fine with watching it on TV.

The Lord explained to me that some of you who are still struggling with smoking have yet to conquer it completely because you still choose to hang around those who smoke. You inhale their secondhand smoke, justifying it by claiming, "Oh, I don't smoke anymore." Some of you feed your clubbing addiction through those friends of yours who go to clubs. Oh, you may not go yourself, but you get together with your buddies and listen to all their raunchy stories, crude jokes, and filthy descriptions of their escapades. Some of you curse no longer, but you intentionally hang around friends who do, and every time they curse, you say nothing about it.

You need to understand that that demon has to be cut off and your flesh-man needs to be starved. Instead of being freed and delivered from the spirit of these sins, you enjoy them secondhand. This is still slavery. This is still bondage.

The Lord told me that some people with homosexual or lesbian traits still hang with other men and women who may have the same traits or who are actual practicing homosexuals or lesbians. This is vicarious exposure to sin, and God says it's time to be freed and delivered and be what He has created you to be as those spirits are designed to strip you of who God designed you to be, because if you do not know who you are, then you will never know your destiny in God

WHAT DOES THIS MEAN FOR YOU?

The short version is you must not yoke yourself together with unbelievers. There is a difference in trying to reach the lost with the gospel and running with them. It is a shame that so many Christians believe that the only real way to reach an unbeliever is to act like them, be like them, and do the things they do. You don't need to be a drunk to reach the drunks.

There is a misunderstanding of a Scripture passage that needs to be addressed here:

For though I be free from all men, yet have I made myself servant unto all, that I might gain the more. And unto the Jews I became as a Jew, that I might gain the Jews; to them that are under the law, as under the law, that I might gain them that are under the law; To them that are without law, as without law, (being not without law to God, but under the law to Christ,) that I might gain them that are without law. To the weak became I as weak, that I might gain the weak: I am made all things to all men, that I might by all means save some. And this I do for the gospel's sake, that I might be partaker thereof with you.

—1 CORINTHIANS 9:19–23

First, notice what Paul did not say. He did not say he became a drug addict to reach the drug addicts. He did not say that he became a liar to reach the liars. He did not say that he became a murderer to reach the murderers. Even the conception of such an argument is folly.

Paul put himself in the shoes of those he was trying to reach so that he could understand them better. He approached a Jew differently than he approached a Gentile. He put himself in the Jew's shoes to understand the Jew so he could reach the Jew. He put himself in the Gentile's shoes to understand the Gentile so he could reach the Gentile.

There is no indication that Paul indulged in sin to reach the sinner. In fact, the sinner is not looking for hope in sin. He is looking for something that he is not. What hope does another sinner offer? Hope must come from somewhere else.

In dealing with unbelievers, your strongest position is one of righteousness. Fuel the spirit of righteousness and bring the gospel to the lost, but don't join in with the unbeliever. Never become part of what they are doing, for you risk transferring the evil spirits upon them to yourself.

First John 4:1 commands us to try or put to the test every spirit that we encounter. When is the last time you put the spirits of your friends to the test? When is the last time you resisted an evil spirit that lay upon a friend?

That's the trouble. Once they are friends, we have accepted their spirits. We have allowed those spirits access to our lives and our families. Once they are friends, they are already influencing you.

Let them become your friends in righteousness, but never become their friends in sin. The transfer of spirits can work both ways, but it depends on which spirit is being promoted. Are you indulging in secondhand sin? Are you yoked with unbelievers, becoming in agreement with those who defy Christ, defy God, defy righteousness?

What business does a believer have with an unbeliever? How can they walk together except they be agreed?

Are you in agreement with unbelievers? What evil spirits have you accepted into your life?

Chapter 8
SOCIAL TRAPS

Ye adulterers and adulteresses, know ye not
that the friendship of the world is enmity
with God? whosoever therefore will be a
friend of the world is the enemy of God.
—JAMES 4:4

OD CREATED US to be sociable creatures. We need people. God never meant for us to go through life without interaction with other people. We are created with needs that only another person can fill in our lives.

When God saw all that He had created, He said it was very good. However, the first time God mentioned that something wasn't good was when He made note that man was alone:

> And the LORD God said, It is not good that the man should be alone; I will make him an help meet for him.
> —GENESIS 2:18

It wasn't good that Adam didn't have someone else to talk to, to relate to, to touch, to enjoy a sunset with, to share experiences with, or to love. God created Eve for so much more than the potential to procreate. He wanted Adam to have someone to socialize with—someone other than God.

At first glance, that statement almost sounds sacrilegious. After all, we only need God, right? God didn't think so. God and Adam had a time of fellowship, but Adam could never be on God's level, so God gave him someone equal to him, someone he could interact with and socialize with.

Socialization is a fundamental aspect of our makeup. Building relationships is essential to our spiritual, emotional, and mental development. In fact, I would dare say that God meant our earthly, godly relationships to be the true source of our earthly happiness. True joy can only come from God, but happiness can be derived from our earthly relationships.

The enemy will try to pervert that socialization need. He will try to twist it, make it something evil and detrimental to your spiritual growth. To that end, he has developed a variety of social traps that are designed to pervert and introduce evil spirits into your relationships.

Too often, we see these traps as just harmless activities to enjoy with friends and family. What we don't see are the influencing spirits that we invite into our lives. There are many social traps, but let's discuss three rather prominent ones.

Drinking

The consumption of alcohol is one of the most debated topics in Christianity. There are some who believe that any amount of drinking is acceptable since we live "under grace" and not under the "law." Others think that we can drink as long as it is in moderation. And still others believe that any form of alcoholic consumption is wrong.

When the topic comes up, most Christians who drink refer to two particular passages of Scripture in attempts to justify their alcoholic consumption. The first, and perhaps most famous, is Jesus turning the water into wine.

John 2 details this miracle. Jesus attended a feast, and

while there, the wedding party ran out of wine. He transformed some water into wine to the astonishment of the
servants and the bafflement of the guests.

However, the term *wine* in the Old and New Testaments
is used for both grape juice and fermented grape juice. The
words "grape juice" are not found in the Bible as all juice
that came from a grape, regardless of its alcoholic content,
was referred to as wine. Since fresh grape juice was difficult to maintain and preserve, it was often considered the
"best" wine. Jesus simply turned the water into grape juice.
The second is found in Ephesians:

> And be not drunk with wine, wherein is excess; but
> be filled with the Spirit.
> —EPHESIANS 5:18

The logic states that as long as you don't get drunk, then
alcoholic consumption is acceptable. This is the moderation perspective.

Alcohol has traditionally and historically been the bev-
erage of choice at social gatherings. It loosens inhibitions
and the tongue, making it the "perfect" social drink.

But let's look at it from a different perspective. To begin
with, everything good that God has, the enemy has a coun-
terfeit for. Everything that God meant for you to enjoy in
this life, the enemy will attempt to pervert.

Another common name for alcoholic beverages is
"spirits." That in itself should tell you everything. If even
the world recognizes that alcohol is spiritual and can have
spiritual effects, then that should sound all sorts of alarms
in your head.

People claim to be "under the influence" of alcohol.
And it is true! They are. They have invited an influencing
spirit into their bodies and they have allowed themselves

to be under the influence of those spirits. People under the influence will say things they don't mean, do things they would not normally do, and risk what they would normally not risk.

Even the Bible contrasts the power of the Holy Spirit to that of the spirit of alcohol:

> And be not drunk with wine, wherein is excess; but be filled with the Spirit.
>
> —EPHESIANS 5:18

> But Peter, standing up with the eleven, lifted up his voice, and said unto them, Ye men of Judaea, and all ye that dwell at Jerusalem, be this known unto you, and hearken to my words: For these are not drunken, as ye suppose, seeing it is but the third hour of the day. But this is that which was spoken by the prophet Joel; And it shall come to pass in the last days, saith God, I will pour out of my Spirit upon all flesh: and your sons and your daughters shall prophesy, and your young men shall see visions, and your old men shall dream dreams.
>
> —ACTS 2:14–17

We are meant to find our love from the Holy Spirit, not from a bottle. We are meant to find joy from the Holy Spirit, not from a beer. We are meant to find peace from the Holy Spirit, not from a martini (Gal. 5:22).

The very reason people drink and all that they want from it is something that the Holy Spirit is supposed to provide us. Instead of turning to the Holy Spirit for these things, many Christians have turned to evil spirits—counterfeits.

Alcohol is a social trap. It lures us in and then entraps us in its snare. Instead of finding that love, joy, and peace that we want, we end up allowing demonic spirits access to our lives.

The command in Ephesians 5:18 is to be filled with the Holy Spirit, not alcohol. The two are mutually exclusive and diametrically opposed to each other. You can't have both.

In the last several years, there has been an increase in the clergy who have been arrested for DUIs. Christians have justified their use of alcohol and we are paying for it. How can the Holy Spirit have reign in our lives when we are under the influence of demonic ones?

SMOKING AND TOBACCO

Smoking is also a social trap. Not only is it highly addictive, but it is largely a legal drug that most people, in the beginning, indulged in because they had a friend or a family member who smoked. The vast majority of smokers smoke because they were around someone who did.

Can a Christian smoke and still walk in the power of the Holy Spirit and have a right relationship with God? Absolutely not.

Our bodies are the temple of God. The Holy Spirit indwells believers, but when we pump the temple full of a substance that corrupts, then we have defiled the temple of God.

> Know ye not that ye are the temple of God, and that the Spirit of God dwelleth in you? If any man defile the temple of God, him shall God destroy; for the temple of God is holy, which temple ye are.
> —1 CORINTHIANS 3:16–17

Note that God promises to destroy him that defiles the temple of God. Is there any wonder that smoking causes cancer? Is it any wonder that a host of diseases and health problems directly stem from smoking? Not according to those verses.

It is usually harder to get someone to stop smoking than it is to stop taking cocaine or alcohol. Once hooked, they rely upon the cigarette to calm their nerves, get them through tough times, and to ease their minds. Again, is this not what the Holy Spirit of God is supposed to do? Why then do we rush to tobacco to do what the Holy Spirit is to do?

It is because of the spirit of addiction. Social traps are designed to send you down the road of an addiction where the addiction becomes your love, your priority, where you spend your money, what you turn to when you are depressed or lonely, and what you rely upon when you are anxious.

Instead of God, you will run to your addiction.

Gambling and Casinos

Over the last twenty years, there has been an increase in attendance at casinos across America by church groups. The enemy is cunning and crafty when it comes to gambling. The lure of easy money, heady entertainment, laughter, and socialization make the average casino a significant social trap for demonic spirits—particularly spirits of addiction.

The spirit of indulgence is a partner spirit in this endeavor. The gambling environment encourages you to indulge in your lusts and passions—alcohol, sex, and love of money. Another spirit that is rife in casinos is the spirit of waste. Let me explain.

God uses money as a benchmark to see where our heart is. According to Matthew 6:21, your heart always follows where you spend your money. But it is more than that. Your money, in most cases, represents your life. So where you spend your money is where you spend your life. God watches where your money goes because He knows that your heart and life follow your money.

Let me see if I can elaborate. Let's say that you work a job making $10 an hour and you get paid for one hour's worth of work. Now you take that $10 and run down to the local casino and spend an hour wasting it on the slot machines. No matter how you attempt to justify it, you have wasted two (2) hours of your life at the casino—the hour you spent earning the $10 and the hour you spent at the casino.

You have indulged in the spirit of waste, indulgence, and possibly addiction. Even if you happen to win (which is the worst thing that could ever happen to a gambler), you have still wasted your life there for ill-gotten gains.

Luck is a false god that is worshiped at casinos. You roll the dice a certain way because you believe it is lucky. You sit a certain way, stand a certain way, play a certain number, rub the cards a particular way, or wear a particular charm all in the hopes of winning big. This is nothing less than idolatry.

Even when you play the lottery, the odds are (the pun is intentional) that you choose certain numbers that you feel are lucky. It is an idolatrous attitude that exhibits demonic spirits in your life.

Instead of faith and trust in God, you turn to the goddess of luck for your security and potential happiness. You worship at her tables, do her bidding, and make sacrifices to her greed all in the hopes that she will bless you with a big payoff one day.

> But ye are they that forsake the LORD, that forget my holy mountain, that prepare a table for that troop, and that furnish the drink offering unto that number.
>
> —Isaiah 65:11

The word *number* is the Hebrew word *meni*. It is the word for fate or luck. The verse is speaking of those who have forsaken the Lord in favor of luck or fate. It is interesting that the King James translators used the word "number" here as if this concept is closely tied to luck or fortune.

God's anger is shown in the next verse as well as His sarcasm:

> Therefore will I number you to the sword, and ye shall all bow down to the slaughter: because when I called, ye did not answer; when I spake, ye did not hear; but did evil before mine eyes, and did choose that wherein I delighted not.
>
> —Isaiah 65:12

In this verse, the word *number* is a different Hebrew word that indicates being appointed to. God clearly views any inclination toward fortune or luck to be idolatry.

You may think that it is no big deal. You may even believe that the money you lose there was yours to lose—and as long as you do it in moderation, then there is no real problem. But you have allowed the spirits of indulgence, waste, and addiction to influence your life.

It is idolatry.

WHAT DOES THIS MEAN FOR YOU?

The smartest thing you can do is control your social settings. Don't indulge in something that will introduce you to evil spirits. Don't go someplace to socialize and introduce seducing spirits, spirits of addiction, spirits of waste, and spirits of indulgence into your life.

There are many social traps that the enemy has laid to snare your life, defile the temple of God, and to enslave your mind. As important as it is to socialize and be around other people, it is more important that you choose wisely both the people you socialize with and the atmosphere in which you socialize.

Whoever is in control of the atmosphere controls the influence. This is so important to learn. When you go to the casino, a bar, a party, or even a movie, you are not in control of the atmosphere. Someone else is. Whatever spirits the person in control brings is the spirit that will be the dominate influence.

If you are a believer and you have the Holy Spirit within you, then you need to control the social settings—or at least go where another godly Christian has control of the atmosphere.

Chapter 9
VISUAL ENTERTAINMENT

Now the Spirit speaketh expressly, that in the latter times some shall depart from the faith, giving heed to seducing spirits, and doctrines of devils.
—1 TIMOTHY 4:1

Train up a child in the way he should go: and when he is old, he will not depart from it.
—PROVERBS 22:6

THE ENEMY IS relentless and unwavering in his desire to corrupt us, and he doesn't just wait for us to become adult before he begins. In truth, he begins when we are mere children. The enemy is determined to preach his doctrine to our children.

God gives a command—a warning perhaps—to parents. He says in Proverbs 22:6, "Train up a child in the way he should go: and when he is old, he will not depart from it." This verse presents a profound truth about children. The best time to train them in righteousness and holiness is when they are young. Those lessons in their youth stick with them for the rest of their lives. They are impressionable, malleable, and trusting.

Unfortunately, the enemy knows this as well. He knows that the best opportunity he has to corrupt a person is in their youth. If he can invade the minds of our children with his doctrine and seduce them while young, then he has a wonderful opportunity to corrupt their minds while they are still open and receptive.

As adults, much of our current belief system and

worldview is predicated on the events and teachings of our youth. Even if we don't hold exactly to a particular philosophy, the teachings, along with particular events, have influenced the belief structure we eventually formed as adults.

This is the reason why God commanded the children of Israel: "And thou shalt teach them diligently unto thy children, and shalt talk of them when thou sittest in thine house, and when thou walkest by the way, and when thou liest down, and when thou risest up" (Deut. 6:7). God knew that each generation needed to be retrained and retaught.

In fact, the children of Israel failed to obey this command. In the Book of Judges, we learn that the people followed the Lord so long as Joshua and the elders that outlived Joshua were still alive. But when they were gone, the children of Israel began worshipping devils and idols.

The enemy is after our children. He is out to corrupt and defile their minds, thinking, and hearts. He wants to begin the process of seducing them away from the things of the Lord at a young age.

One of the tools he uses is television. TV is insidious. Follow the logic. If an unmarried couple knocks on your door and asks if they can borrow your couch so they can have sex—and no, they wouldn't mind if you and your children watched—you would slam the door in their face. Instead, we turn on the TV and watch it right there while sitting on said couch. In fact, too often we invite sinful behavior right into our living rooms and bedrooms via the TV.

That, of course, is a blatant and perhaps extreme example for some, but the enemy is a lot more subtle than that. As parents, we would naturally not allow our children to watch a sex scene. Instead, we sit them down before cartoons. After all, cartoons are innocent, aren't they?

Let's examine that claim.

Cartoons

I remember waking up on a Saturday morning and rushing into the living room as a boy and excitedly plopping myself down before the TV to watch cartoons. As a child, I didn't have the discernment to examine the content or the context of the cartoons I watched. To me, I just loved the action. I would sit for hours, absorbing every image, every sound that my parents would allow.

As I matured both naturally and spiritually, I discovered the horrible truth surrounding most cartoon shows. In prayer, the Lord showed me that the enemy is seeking to infiltrate our children by utilizing seemingly innocuous demonic induced suggestions over infiltrated airwaves.

My favorite cartoon back then was called *He-Man*. This cartoon depicted a boy who could transform himself into a superhero with bulging muscles. He would raise his power sword and shout, "By the power of Greyskull, I have the power!" Instantly, he would be transformed. I would run around the house chanting this slogan and vanquishing imaginary enemies with my imaginary superhuman strength.

What I didn't know was that I was invoking a demonic ritual and opening myself up to demonic impartations. You might be wondering how that could be, but the answer is simple. This cartoon was subtly teaching me that I didn't need God, that power and might came from me, not my Creator. I had the power. I just needed to invoke it. This is so contrary to what Jesus said in Matthew 28:18, "All power is given unto me in heaven and earth." According to that verse, Jesus has all the power! In my little fantasy mind, however, I wasn't turning to Jesus for power, but to Greyskull—a picture of death. It was subtle, it was slow, but it did have an impact on my young and impressionable mind.

Think about many of the cartoons out there. How many of them have fairies, demons, magic, and supernatural elements that are contrary to God? It seems like most do.

Some of you may recall the cartoon Smurfs. Smurfs was a society of little blue men—and only one female. In a subtle way, this taught homosexual concepts to our children. The main villains in the story were named after principle demons. Even though these villains were portrayed as evil, their names became common household names to many children. How is this good?

The Power Rangers invoked qualities of magic, specifically elemental magic such as earth, air, fire, and water to gain magical power. The animated series *Avatar* also utilized elemental magic in their martial arts. In *Voltron*, the cartoon about the various metal lions each represented one of the elements that gave them their individual powers. The "loveable" Dora the Explorer used incantations and dark magic.

Interestingly, many of the cartoons I mentioned were ones from my own childhood. They have not gotten better in this day and age!

All of these cartoons simply indoctrinate our children into a real or even fantasy world where God is not supreme, where power comes from within or from the earth, where alternative lifestyles are accepted, and where scantily clad women with large breasts and heavily muscled men solve all their problems with violence.

We wonder where our children learn about sex and sexuality, but all we need to do is watch their cartoons with them and we'll have no doubt where they are getting much of it from. Look at the interaction between the characters. Look at how the characters are dressed and what body parts are accentuated. Listen to the words and sexual innuendos.

But even seemingly innocent animated movies such as *The Land Before Time* utilize a godless theme of "follow your heart." Sounds good, but the Bible is very clear that the heart is desperately wicked (Jer. 17:9) and to follow it is complete foolishness (Prov. 28:26).

We must remember that these children's cartoons and movies are not made by Christians. They are generally made by godless men and women promoting a worldly or even demonic worldview. By allowing these shows into our homes, we are inviting demonic spirits to influence our children and families. It is very dangerous.

TV SHOWS AND MOVIES

Entertainment is big industry. It is a billion dollar industry, and Satan has his fingers all over it. Someone once said that you will be the same person in five years as you are now except for the people you know and the books you read. I would add something else to that list...except for the TV you watch.

Any film producer knows that a movie carries a message. It might be covert or overt, but you cannot watch a TV show or a movie without being subjected to the "message" of the show. You may think it is just entertainment—good fun—but it is neither good nor righteous entertainment.

Let me list some of the hazards of watching movies and TV shows:

1. Vicarious enjoyment of sin and decadence
2. The unconscious acceptance of the message
3. The desensitization to sin and violence
4. The invitation of demonic spirits into your life and home

Let's take them one at a time.

Vicarious Enjoyment of Sin and Decadence

Many Christians will not go out and kill someone. They will not sleep with someone who is not their spouse. They will not curse or swear. They will not lie or cheat. They will not try to hurt someone.

But they don't mind watching it.

This vicarious enjoyment of sin is deceptive. We think that because it isn't real, it doesn't matter. But it does. It affects your thinking, your outlook, and your willingness to accept the unacceptable.

The spirit of confusion begins to work in your life. Have you ever watched a child after watching a martial arts movie? What does he do? He runs around the house pretending to beat everyone up. What does a child do after watching Superman? Gets himself a cape and jumps off the couch. What do you think is going on in his mind when he watches two people in a sexual position? What goes on in your mind?

What is it that you fantasize about after watching your favorite TV show? Oh, you may not run around wearing a cape anymore, but your mind has been invaded by the spirit of that show. Where does your mind go?

The psalmist said:

> I will set no wicked thing before mine eyes: I hate the work of them that turn aside; it shall not cleave to me.
>
> —Psalm 101:3

The psalmist understood that to accept something vicariously, he would have to watch it. To avoid that, he refused to watch anything he would not participate in himself. In fact, he said he hated the works of those that turn aside from the truth.

How about you?

The Unconscious Acceptance of the Message

When we watch a movie, we subject ourselves to the message of the show. We may disagree with it, but we have allowed it to have its say. We gave it a platform. We gave it access to our minds and hearts.

Homosexuality has become the darling of the movie industry. It is now common to find homosexual partners, marriages, and situations portrayed in movies. Indeed, they are portrayed as something good and wholesome and those who oppose it as bigoted and evil. You may disagree with that message, but you allowed the message into your home and into your mind.

We are warned about this in the Bible:

> Neither give place to the devil.
>
> —Ephesians 4:27

The word *place* implies a location, a platform, a medium. We are not to allow the devil a platform to deliver his messages to our lives. I understand that you may feel you mentally, emotionally, and even spiritually disagree with many of the messages portrayed in TV shows, but this isn't about your agreement. This is about the fact that you allowed the enemy to deliver his message to you—and you sat there and listened to it! Your TV is a medium, a platform by which you allow messages to be "preached" to you through visual and audio methods.

Would you allow a Satanist to come in and teach your family about dark magic? No, but in the name of entertainment, you will allow a TV show to do so. Take Harry Potter for example.

Harry Potter taught an entire generation of children that witches, magic, goblins, dragons, wizards, and sorcery are good things. You would never send your children to a school to learn magic, but then you didn't need to either. You could just let them watch Harry Potter.

By allowing those shows into your home, you allowed the spirit of confusion to be preached to you.

The Desensitization to Sin and Violence

There is a very interesting warning given in the Bible. I mentioned part of it at the beginning of this chapter. Now, let's look at the entire warning:

> Now the Spirit speaketh expressly, that in the latter times some shall depart from the faith, giving heed to seducing spirits, and doctrines of devils; Speaking lies in hypocrisy; having their conscience seared with a hot iron.
> —1 TIMOTHY 4:1–2

TV is without a doubt a seducing spirit preaching the doctrine of devils. But notice verse 2. It speaks of a seared conscience. No longer does this individual see things as wrongly as he once did. No more does he find what he sees on the TV as abhorrent. In fact, he has even begun to rationalize and justify it.

It's just entertainment, right? We can handle it. It doesn't affect us. This is nothing more than a hypocritical lie.

Here is a little test you can take to prove that you have become desensitized to sin by the amount of TV you watch. Stop watching all TV for two months. Then start again. If you have kept your mind on pure things for those two months, you will be shocked at the amount of cussing, lewdness, sex, and violence there is when you start watching again. You can become so desensitized to things like cussing that you don't even realize that they even cussed. What does that say for the state of your spirit?

When you allow sin to inflict your soul each and every day, you become desensitized to it. Lot did this. Notice the following verses:

> And delivered just Lot, vexed with the filthy conversation of the wicked: (For that righteous man dwelling among them, in seeing and hearing, vexed his righteous soul from day to day with their unlawful deeds;).
> —2 PETER 2:7–8

Lot eventually became numb to it all. It didn't bother him. In fact, he even moved into Sodom and allowed the culture to corrupt his children. Lot himself never converted to it, but he did become desensitized to it. And it destroyed him and his family.

What is your TV destroying in your life and in your family? What has it destroyed, but you are numb to its loss?

Demonic Invitation

Let's look at a verse again:

> Now the Spirit speaketh expressly, that in the latter
> times some shall depart from the faith, giving heed
> to seducing spirits, and doctrines of devils.
>
> —1 TIMOTHY 4:1

As stated in the last point, TV is the way we have come to give heed (to listen to) seducing spirits and doctrines of devils. We have not only given Satan a platform to preach his doctrine to our hearts and family, but we have allowed the seducing spirit to do so right in our own homes!

The TV, in most homes, has a prominent location. It is not even hidden or watched in secret. We allow it to take up a significant portion of our home and of our lives. We have given the enemy an invitation to our homes.

Don't ignore this warning! We've given place to the devil and we will reap the consequences. If you don't think that TV is being used by the enemy, then you have become self-deluded.

WHAT DOES THIS MEAN FOR YOU?

In short, it means the safest thing to do is get rid of the TV. I will be the first to admit that there are good shows and even Christian shows that we can safely watch. However, the vast majority of the programs on TV are nothing more than a soapbox for the enemy.

Control the TV. Don't let it control you.

It isn't even just the movies themselves you have to be careful of. The commercials have become nothing more than sensual attempts at capturing your heart. You may not drink yourself, but what message is being preached to you and your family when you watch a beer commercial? Why would you even want such a message preached in your home?

It's time we did something about this one-eyed demon that sits so stately in a place of honor in our homes. It is time we turned the thing off!

Chapter 10
BREAKING FREE

*Stand fast therefore in the liberty wherewith
Christ hath made us free, and be not entangled again with the yoke of bondage.*

—GALATIANS 5:1

REAKING FREE FROM the yoke of bondage should be
the goal of any right-thinking believer. When we are
held captive by evil spirits, we have severed our fellowship with God, and in such a state, we can have no
peace or joy.

There is a warning to believers in 2 Peter that we must
take heed of:

> For if after they have escaped the pollutions of
> the world through the knowledge of the Lord and
> Saviour Jesus Christ, they are again entangled
> therein, and overcome, the latter end is worse with
> them than the beginning. For it had been better for
> them not to have known the way of righteousness,
> than, after they have known it, to turn from the holy
> commandment delivered unto them.
>
> —2 PETER 2:20–21

This is a strongly worded warning. If you are entangled
as a believer by these seducing spirits, the end result will
be catastrophic. In fact, he goes on to say that it is almost
better that you had never been freed from these evil spirits
than to be freed and then become entangled in bondage
again.

So what can you do? Here are a few practical strategies that can help us break free of the bondage of these evil spirits.

BE REAL

Most people will deny that they are indulging in sin, and with this mind-set, God can't help or deliver you from the clutches of the enemy.

It is not easy to admit your wrongdoing, but confessing your sin is essential to jump-starting the spiritual cleansing that must take place in order to be freed from spiritual bondage. Notice the following verse:

> If we confess our sins, he is faithful and just to forgive us our sins, and to cleanse us from all unrighteousness.
>
> —1 JOHN 1:9

The cleansing of unrighteousness in our life cannot begin until confession and admission of the sin takes place. So be real to yourself and to God. It's not as if God doesn't already know. Pretending you don't have a problem does not change the reality.

This leads right into my second point.

OUTWARDLY CONFESS AND REBUKE YOUR SIN

Outwardly confessing your sin is essential to the process of being freed from bondage. Not only do you need to admit it to yourself, you need to verbally rebuke the sin. Confessing your sin is a start, but there needs to be more than an admission. There needs to be a rebuking of the sin.

Our confession of sin, I fear, is much like a child *told* to say, "I'm sorry," after having slugged his brother. He may say it, but he doesn't really mean it and will most likely slug his brother again when he is irritated. You may confess your sin, but until you rebuke the sin in your life, it may be that you really didn't mean it.

Take the sin to task. Name it. Denounce your own participation in it. Apologize and ask God to deliver you from it.

Don't forget that sin is always accompanied by spiritual influences. Every time you allow sin to reign in your life, you give permission to these spirits to dominate and control your life. To be free of them, they must be rebuked... not just the sin, but the spirit behind the sin.

REMOVE ALL SIN ITEMS FROM YOUR LIFE

As discussed in a previous chapter, it is important that you rid your life of those items that evil spirits may have attached themselves to. These could be gifts from people who have allowed seducing spirits to dominate their lives to items that are used specifically to indulge in sin—such as a pipe, a TV, a computer, a book, anything.

These things can retain the lingering spirit of the sin that the item was used to perpetuate. Allowing them to remain in your life will not only remind you of the sinful activity, but will allow the spirit of that sin to influence your mind and the minds of those in the house with you.

The Holy Spirit will give you direction here, but only if you are walking in the Spirit.

ATTEND CHURCH

There are many reasons why you should attend church. One that is rarely discussed is the corporate strength that can be gained from church attendance. When you are around fellow believers who are walking in the Spirit, you are allowing the Holy Spirit to influence your life and the lives of your family.

Notice what God said in Hebrews:

> And let us consider one another to provoke unto love and to good works: Not forsaking the assembling of ourselves together, as the manner of some is; but exhorting one another: and so much the more, as ye see the day approaching.
>
> —Hebrews 10:24–25

The closer we get to Christ's return, the more we need each other, fellow brothers and sisters in Christ. We need to be assembling (churching) together. Don't forsake your fellow brothers and sisters in Christ. You need them.

Church allows godly influences to have an impact on your life.

Plan to Win

Without a plan, you will fail. There are too many traps and spiritual black holes in the world that you can get sucked into. With a plan, however, you can avoid them.

> For though we walk in the flesh, we do not war after the flesh: (For the weapons of our warfare are not carnal, but mighty through God to the pulling down of strong holds;) Casting down imaginations, and every high thing that exalteth itself against the knowledge of God, and bringing

into captivity every thought to the obedience of Christ.

—2 CORINTHIANS 10:3–5

The weapons we have are God's Word and prayer. Immerse yourself in God's Word and arm yourself with prayer. Each day of your life, get up in the morning, read God's Word, and then pray for the day.

When you got up this morning, what was your plan to not fall into sin? What were you planning on doing to defeat the enemy and be victorious in Christ? Did you have a plan? Make sure you do for tomorrow.

Allow Jesus to grow in your life.

FIGHT!

The Word of God declares that if we resist the devil, he will flee from us:

> Submit yourselves therefore to God. Resist the devil, and he will flee from you.
>
> —JAMES 4:7

Don't give up. Don't get discouraged. You don't need to fight by your own power and strength. You don't need to carry the burden of the battle yourself. Rely upon Jesus Christ! He will fight for you!

> Put on the whole armour of God, that ye may be able to stand against the wiles of the devil. For we wrestle not against flesh and blood, but against principalities, against powers, against the rulers of the darkness of this world, against spiritual wickedness in high places. Wherefore take unto you the whole armour of God, that ye may be able to

withstand in the evil day, and having done all, to stand.

—EPHESIANS 6:11–13

We have access to the armor of God. You don't need to stand against the devil alone.

Don't let the enemy win!

ABOUT THE AUTHOR

As an ordained minister for over fifteen years, Dr. Edward Johnson ThD has devoted his adulthood to helping people see the light that Christ can bring into their lives. With the backing of his doctorate in theology and his passion for Christ, he is able to deliver people from the hands and clutches of the enemy on a daily basis.

In addition to spreading God's word to the masses, Dr. Johnson is the current CEO of a major technology-based company. When he's not busy working, Dr. Johnson loves to spend time with his loving and supportive wife, Amber, and his two beautiful and vivacious children, Krystal and Edward Johnson III.

CONTACT THE AUTHOR

Website:
www.demonicwarfare.com

Booking:
Booking@demonicwarfare.com

Interviews:
contact@demonicwarfare.com

Information:
contact@demonicwarfare.com

Facebook:
www.facebook.com/demonicwarfare.com